نوروزتان پیروز !

A Journey to Nowruz

By Taraneh

2025

To my son, Journey!

*Your journey's to find the best you can be,
And I'm here beside you, in all ways you'll need.*

Nowruz comes from Persian hearts
3,000 years ago, a timeless start

World oldest festival, it's true
Millions celebrate like me and you!

On Nowruz, the first day of spring
The earth wakes up, and the birds all sing!

**Nanna winter is ready to go,
winter ends with the melting snow**

Uncle Nowruz plays his Sorna,
Bringing spring with joy hurrah!

Chaharshanbe Soori, fire is bright,
Say goodbye to dark, hello to light!

The last Wednesday night, we celebrate
"Give me your red, take my pale" we say

**Khane Tekani, Clean to shine
A fresh, clean home feels so fine!**

We go shopping full of cheer,
Wearing new things as the new year's near!

Haft-Sin Table with the seven S
It's mgical in every way!

The Seven S's

Sabzeh:
Green and fresh sprouts grow,
For a year that blooms and glows!

Seeb:
A red and shiny apple,
Brings good health to all we meet!

The Seven S's

Seer:
Garlic strong, keeps away
All the bad things, night and day!

Senjed:
Dried oleaster is so sweet,
Brings more love to all we meet!

The Seven S's

Samanu:
A wheat pudding soft and yummy,
A sweet new year for every tummy!

Serkeh:
vinegar, sour and wise,
Teaches us to open our eyes!

The Seven S's

Sumac:
A red spice like a sunrise bright,
Brings new beginnings,
fresh and right!

Candles glow and flowers grow
A Hafez book with poems to know!

Kids get Eidi and money too,
A happy start for something new!

We visit or call to say hello,
Hugs and kisses make love grow!

Sizdah Bedar is Picnic Time!
On day thirteen, we have fun!

Happy Nowruz!

About Nowruz !

The first Nowruz celebrations likely took place in Persepolis!

About Nowruz!

Nowruz means "New Day" in Persian.

تبریک نوروز

نوروز مبارک

عید نوروز بر شما مبارک باشد

سال نو مبارک

نوروزتان پیروز

Nowruz congratulations!

Happy Nowruz!
May the Nowruz holiday
-be blessed for you!
Happy New Year!
May your Nowruz be victorious!

Let's color together!

Copyright © 2015 Taraneh Karimi

All rights reserved.
No part of this book may be reproduced, stored in a retrieval system, or transmitted in any form or by any means, electronic, mechanical, photocopying, recording, or otherwise, without prior written permission from the author or publisher, except for the use of brief quotations in a review.

For permissions, contact: taranehstudio.com

A Persian poem about Nowruz
by Saadi Shirazi:

برخیز که می‌رود زمستان

بگشای در سرای بستان

**Rise, for winter is departing,
Open the doors to the garden's delight.**

Made in the USA
Las Vegas, NV
19 March 2025